MUSHROOM
RECIPES

MUSHROOM RECIPES

COLLECTED BY

André L. Simon

INTRODUCTION BY
F. C. ATKINS
*Chairman of the Mushroom Growers'
Association of Great Britain
and Northern Ireland*

DOVER PUBLICATIONS, INC.
NEW YORK

TO COMPTON MACKENZIE

TX
804
.S5
1975

This Dover edition, first published in 1975, is an unabridged and unaltered republication of the work first published in 1951 by Newman Neame under the title *Mushrooms Galore*.

International Standard Book Number: 0-486-20913-X
Library of Congress Catalog Card Number: 74-15001

Manufactured in the United States of America
Dover Publications, Inc.
180 Varick Street
New York, N. Y. 10014

CONTENTS

INTRODUCTION   7

MUSHROOMS GALORE!   10

HOW TO COOK MUSHROOMS   12
Clayton Hutton's way   13   Blanche Hulton's way   13

SOME OF THE MORE POPULAR WAYS of cooking mushrooms

1	Baked mushrooms English Style	14	7 Champignons flambés	15
2	Baked mushrooms French Style	14	8 Fried mushrooms	15
3	Broiled mushrooms	14	9 Mushrooms au Gratin	16
4	Casserole mushrooms	14	10 Grilled mushrooms	16
5	Creamed mushrooms	15	11 Mushrooms sur le plat	16
6	Devilled mushrooms	15	12 Mushrooms Purée	16
			13 Stewed mushrooms	17

SOME MUSHROOM SAUCES, STUFFINGS & GARNITURES

14	Sauce Chasseur	18	21 Mushroom sauce New Style	20
15	Duxelles	18	22 Mushroom sauce for oysters	20
16	Sauce Financière	18	23 Sauce Provençale	20
17	Ketchup or Catsup	18	24 Sauce Régence	20
18	Sauce Madère	19	25 Mushroom stuffings	21
19	Garniture Milanaise	19	26 Sauce Victoria	21
20	Mushroom sauce Old Style	19		

SOME BASIC SAUCES USED FOR MUSHROOM RECIPES

27	Allemande	22	32	Piquante		24
28	Béarnaise	22	33	Poulette		25
29	Béchamel	23	34	Roux		25
30	Espagnole or Brown sauce	23	35	Velouté		25
31	Mornay	24				

MUSHROOMS FOR BREAKFAST   27

MUSHROOMS FOR LUNCHEON

36	Salade de Champignons	28	53	Anguille Beaucaire	31
37	Banquettes of mushrooms	28	54	Mackerel à l'italienne	31
38	Bouchées aux champignons	28	55	Matelote	32
39	Canapés Pauline	28	56	Baked stuffed smelts	32
40	Champignons au beurre	29	57	Brochettes of kidneys	33
41	Champignons bourgeoise	29	58	Rognons à la berrichonne	33
42	Champignons aux fines herbes	29	59	Fricassée de poulet	33
43	Champignons à la grecque	29	60	Fried chicken Tartare	34
			61	Planked broiler	34
44	Champignons à la hongroise	29	62	Croquettes of chicken	35
45	Champignons à la lyonnaise	29	63	Compote of pigeons	36
			64	Turkey giblets bourgeoise	36
46	Champignons marinés	30	65	Lancashire Hot-Pot	37
47	Champignons à la poulette	30	66	Mixed grill	37
			67	Veau Marengo	37
48	Flan aux champignons	30	68	Blanquette de veau (New Style)	38
49	Omelette aux champignons	30	69	Blanquette de veau (Old Style)	38
50	Omelette aux champignons (Normande)	30	70	Bouilli au gratin	38
			71	Salmis d'agneau	38
51	Noodles with mushrooms	30	72	Escalopes de mouton aux champignons	39
52	Œufs au plat et oeufs au four: Colette; Duxelles;	31	73	Lapin en blanquette	39
	Ermenonville;	31	74	Lapin chasseur	40
	Petit-Duc;	31	75	Le civet de lapin	40
	Saint-Honoré	31	76	Snipe Pudding	41

MUSHROOMS FOR DINNER

77	Mushroom soup	42	94	Filets de truite Vauclusienne	47
78	Green eggs	42	95	Turbot Bonne Femme	48
79	Vol-au-vent surprise	43	96	Tête de veau en tortue	48
80	Chicken liver croustades	44	97	Poulet sauté Marengo	49
81	Rognons de veau Clémentine	44	98	Poulet sauté Portugaise	49
82	Lobster Chow Min	44	99	Stuffed lamb chops	50
83	Stuffed lobster	45	100	Lamb cutlets	
84	Red Mullets with mushrooms	45		Barman	51
				Brossard	51
85	Sole Ambassadrice	45		Montrouge	51
86	Sole Bonne Femme	46	101	Filet de boeuf Bressanne	51
87	Sole Normande	46	102	Filet de boeuf Madère	51
88	Sole au plat	47	103	Tournedos Chasseur	51
89	Sole Provençale	47	104	Tournedos Dauphinoise	51
90	Sole Bourguignonne	47	105	Rumpsteak à la hussarde	52
91	Sole Carême	47	106	Fillets of veal Talleyrand	53
92	Sole Chambord	47	107	Perdreaux en Papillotes	53
93	Sole Coquelin	47	108	Roast Pheasant with mushrooms	53

MUSHROOMS FOR SUPPER

109	Mushroom tarts	54	110	Mushrooms sous cloche	54

CONVERSION TABLES FOR FOREIGN EQUIVALENTS

DRY INGREDIENTS

Ounces		Grams	Grams		Ounces	Pounds		Kilograms	Kilograms		Pounds
1	=	28.35	1	=	0.035	1	=	0.454	1	=	2.205
2		56.70	2		0.07	2		0.91	2		4.41
3		85.05	3		0.11	3		1.36	3		6.61
4		113.40	4		0.14	4		1.81	4		8.82
5		141.75	5		0.18	5		2.27	5		11.02
6		170.10	6		0.21	6		2.72	6		13.23
7		198.45	7		0.25	7		3.18	7		15.43
8		226.80	8		0.28	8		3.63	8		17.64
9		255.15	9		0.32	9		4.08	9		19.84
10		283.50	10		0.35	10		4.54	10		22.05
11		311.85	11		0.39	11		4.99	11		24.26
12		340.20	12		0.42	12		5.44	12		26.46
13		368.55	13		0.46	13		5.90	13		28.67
14		396.90	14		0.49	14		6.35	14		30.87
15		425.25	15		0.53	15		6.81	15		33.08
16		453.60	16		0.57						

LIQUID INGREDIENTS

Liquid Ounces		Milliliters	Milliliters		Liquid Ounces	Quarts		Liters	Liters		Quarts
1	=	29.573	1	=	0.034	1	=	0.946	1	=	1.057
2		59.15	2		0.07	2		1.89	2		2.11
3		88.72	3		0.10	3		2.84	3		3.17
4		118.30	4		0.14	4		3.79	4		4.23
5		147.87	5		0.17	5		4.73	5		5.28
6		177.44	6		0.20	6		5.68	6		6.34
7		207.02	7		0.24	7		6.62	7		7.40
8		236.59	8		0.27	8		7.57	8		8.45
9		266.16	9		0.30	9		8.52	9		9.51
10		295.73	10		0.33	10		9.47	10		10.57

Gallons (American)		Liters	Liters		Gallons (American)
1	=	3.785	1	=	0.264
2		7.57	2		0.53
3		11.36	3		0.79
4		15.14	4		1.06
5		18.93	5		1.32
6		22.71	6		1.59
7		26.50	7		1.85
8		30.28	8		2.11
9		34.07	9		2.38
10		37.86	10		2.74

INTRODUCTION

by

FRED. C. ATKINS

Chairman of the Mushroom Growers' Association and the Mushroom Research Association Ltd.

THE MUSHROOM GROWER rivals the angler in reputation as a teller of far-fetched tales. But it is an attitude he adopts in self-defence, for if you cross-examine him closely he will eventually have to admit that he doesn't even know *why* mushrooms grow. To conceal that ignorance he will talk learnedly of the conditions which discourage growth and his increasing dependence on scientific research. But he'll not be able to say that, if you do this and that, you'll be certain to get mushrooms.

Therein, of course, lies the irresistible fascination of this crop for growers large and small, professional and amateur. A great deal is known about Mushrooms, and the practical experience gained during their cultivation over the past 300 years is not to be discounted; but exactly what factors persuade the mushroom-bed to fruit are not known. Indeed, a distinguished Belgian Professor is this year starting a programme of research concentrated on this one fundamental problem.

We know that a mushroom is a "fungus," a form of plant life which, instead of seeding, produces "spores" underneath its cap on what are called "gills," radiating like the spokes of a wheel. It is the ripening of these spores which causes the underside of the mushroom to change from a delicate shade of pink to chocolate-brown. Although of course, the whole mushroom, including the stalk, is edible it is in the ripe spores that the full flavour is to be found.

The mushroom remains tightly closed while the spores are forming, and then the umbrella is opened to allow them to fall to the ground—which they do, in their millions. Being so small, they are carried away by every breath of air; some have been known to drift many miles. Few germinate, because they are very fussy about their food; they would rather die than accept an unpalatable meal—as the furrowed forehead of every mushroom grower will testify!

If it should happen that a spore does come to rest on some warm decaying vegetable matter which satisfies its exacting demands, it throws out transparent threads which are so delicate that a powerful microscope is needed to see them. These weave in and out, and branch off in all directions in search of food, storing what they find until such time as it is required. The mushroom grower's "spawn" is simply vegetable matter which has been so thoroughly permeated by these threads that it looks and smells (and indeed is) mouldy.

Then, when a number of conditions have been satisfied, or when a fortuitous combination of circumstances gives the All Clear signal, mushrooms start to form. Tiny white balls appear and begin to swell, and then they produce stalks that lift them clear of the ground.

Mushrooms don't grow overnight. In an environment which experience suggests is almost ideal, a couple of months is required for the spore to germinate and for sufficient food to be gathered to sustain its fruit. What we call the mushroom is in fact the fruit of the mushroom organism that lives underground. (Some fungi, such as the Truffle, produce even their fruit underground.) The fruiting body itself takes nearly a week to mature.

In other countries many different kinds of wild mushroom are eaten, but in Great Britain there has been a growing preference for mushrooms which have been "cultivated," under hygienic conditions, and the most popular variety bears the scientific name *Psalliota bispora*. It belongs to the same family as the field mushroom, *Psalliota campestris*, but demands quite different food and produces its spores as twins instead of quads.

The Mushroom grower is frequently asked why he does not cultivate other varieties. The answer, of course, is that centuries of experience have given him the answer to only a handful of the many problems associated with the one *Psalliota bispora* variety, and the growing of it is still a gamble; how, then, dare he tackle other fungi which probably have just as many peculiarities and idiosyncrasies?

There are other reasons, too. The English are conservative in their outlook on food, and shopkeepers would hesitate to stock species which were unknown to their customers. Again, the cultivated mushroom travels well and is fit to eat several days after it has been gathered. The pleasant Fairy Ring Mushroom, on the other hand, is very fragile and would be badly crushed and broken long before it reached the table of town dwellers; and the delicate Inky Cap would present a sorry sight, for it breaks down into a black inky mess within a few hours of reaching maturity.

There would be a ready sale for Truffles, but a lengthy and expensive programme of scientific research would be an essential preliminary to cultivation—and where would the money come from? The mushroom grower is in no position to find it. He spends thousands of pounds every year on research designed to increase his efficiency; that has doubled his output, but it now costs him three times as much as it did ten years ago to produce each pound of mushrooms, and the narrow margin between cost and wholesale price is very near the economic limit. Only through further heavy capital expenditure and still more research can there be any chance of reducing the price of mushrooms in the shops. And if the 1s. a lb. fall experienced during the past three years continues for another 12 months so many commercial growers will be out of business that the law of supply and demand will inevitably assert itself and prices will probably tend to rise again.

FRED. C. ATKINS

MUSHROOMS GALORE

ALL VEGETABLES are good for us, of course, but some are better than others, and there are two which are the best of all: they are Potatoes and Mushrooms. Why best? Because they are with us at all times of the year *fresh*, and in spite of the wonderful achievements in the science of tinning, canning, bottling, dehydrating, and quick-freezing, the freshest foods are still the best. But there is another test by which we can tell the best foods: they are those which we can eat and enjoy every day. Of course, there are millions of Asiatics who eat rice everyday and millions of Africans who eat groundnuts every day; rice and groundnuts are very good foods; so are oats which a horse will be quite content to eat every day. But among the more highly civilized peoples food is not merely fuel shovelled in the boiler to keep the works going: food has to satisfy our senses of sight, smell and taste to give our highly developed nervous system that measure of relaxation and enjoyment which we often need even more than the physiological supply of carbohydrates, proteins and vitamins. Bread and butter, potatoes and mushrooms are among the few foods that are capable of being enjoyed by most if not all of us every day, and they are on that account the best. Parsnips once in a way, with boiled silverside; turnips now and again, with a *ragoût* of duck; a braised Spanish onion on a cold winter's day, or crunchy spring onions with cheese and beer, on a summer's morning; cabbage, carrots, green peas, French beans, celery, artichokes, asparagus, and the rest, in season, are good, very good, excellent, but not the best because we would soon tire of them if we had them day after day, as we have potatoes and as we should have mushrooms every day. The reason for this is quite obvious: neither the plebeian Potato nor the patrician Mushroom has the sweetness of taste of some vegetables which the palate so gladly welcomes and so soon finds a bore; nor the assertiveness of others which may be quite attractive occasionally but are apt to become tiresome when they press their claim upon our attention continually. Potatoes and Mushrooms are neither sweet of taste nor aggressive of flavour: they are admirably discreet and they bear with admirable fortitude the ordeal by fire which prepares them for the table; they never are guilty of the loud plaint that fills the air so malodorously when cabbage is boiled or onions are fried. Both Potatoes and Mushrooms are good mixers, never attempting to eclipse or quarrel with the eggs, fish, flesh or fowl with which they happen to be served: on the contrary, they help them to look better dressed and to taste better.

Mushrooms are, to-day, a luxury, but Potatoes were also a luxury once upon a time, and so was Tea, when it cost Twelve Pounds per pound. A bathroom was also a luxury some sixty years ago, and so was constant hot water, less than thirty years ago. There is no reason why Mushrooms should not gradually pass from the luxury class into that of the necessaries of life. Surely if oranges and bananas can be and are enjoyed by rich and poor alike in this country, where they do not grow, Mushrooms deserve to be equally if not even more popular, since they are grown all the year round in many parts of England. What is needed is a wider appreciation of the value of Mushrooms both as *aliment* and *condiment*, that is nutritionally as food, and gastronomically, for their flavour. A greater demand would mean greater supplies and lower prices. This collection of Mushroom recipes has been made to stimulate the imagination of the housewife, whether she does her own cooking or has a cook to do it for her, so that she may provide for the household fare which Mushrooms will make more tasty and more dainty, not on festive or special occasions only, but every day.

ANDRÉ SIMON

HOW TO COOK MUSHROOMS

THE BEST WAY to cook mushrooms is the way you like best, at the time. There is no way that is best under any and every condition, and matters of taste are not like matters of faith: we all may have a taste of our own, and we are even at liberty to change about whenever we happen to be in the mood for a change without anybody having any right to accuse us of heresy. There are experts, however, who claim that their way of cooking Mushrooms is the *Best*, and the first two recipes that we shall give in the own words of their authors illustrate how experts can differ. The only way for each one of us to make up our mind which is the better method of the two, is to try them both in turn and the proof will be in the Mushrooms.

It is important to bear in mind that the little 'button' mushrooms have no more flavour than the tightly closed rose bud has scent, but they have their uses as garnishings and otherwise. It is only when the Mushroom is 'ripe' or fully open that it has all its flavour to give us.

TWO RECIPES

Mushrooms are so delicate that they can be ruined in the cooking. After trying many ways I found that to get the best flavour from mushrooms, you should not under any circumstances peel them. I do not know what my French friends will say to that, but I write from personal experience, and I know that all who have tried my way will have no other. The best way with mushrooms, to my mind, is to put them in a colander, umbrellas upwards, after cutting off the stalks flush (of course, the stalks should on no account be thrown away but put in a pot for soup or sauce). Pour slowly about three kettles of boiling water over the mushrooms in the colander. This will soften the skins. You should never take the skin off; if you do, you remove the best of the mushroom fragrance, and that is why I never grew them above four inches across—then the skin was not tough. After this, take them out and turn them upside down in a Pyrex. Cover them with fresh butter and gently simmer at a steady heat for twenty minutes. On serving, and *only on serving*, pour a little good cream over them. If there is anything more delicious, I have never eaten it.

W. CLAYTON HUTTON'S RECIPE

Mushrooms should be skinned and placed *stalks uppermost* in a greased dish with a small dab of butter or margarine to each mushroom, and cooked till tender, always keeping the lid on the dish in which they are cooked and serving in the same dish; they are far more delicate in flavour and more tender than when either grilled or chopped up. The secret of all the most delicious mushroom dishes is to keep the cover on the dish when cooking and to serve the mushrooms in the dish in which they have been cooked.

BLANCHE HULTON'S RECIPE

SOME OF THE MORE POPULAR WAYS OF COOKING MUSHROOMS

BAKED MUSHROOMS (ENGLISH STYLE)
: Remove the stems and peel the caps of bought mushrooms; if young, freshly-picked mushrooms, wash the outside of the caps, but do not peel them. Place in a baking-dish, the gills up; sprinkle pepper and salt and a very little pounded mace, if liked. Put a small pat of butter on each cap and bake for 20 or 25 minutes, according to size of caps. Serve in the dish in which they were cooked, with a light dusting of coralline pepper.

BAKED MUSHROOMS (FRENCH STYLE)
: Clean the mushrooms, peeling or not, according to whether quite freshly-picked or not; if just gathered, they need only wiping or washing. Remove the stalks and cook the caps slowly in pork fat or olive oil for two or three minutes only; take them out and place them in a fireproof dish. In the meantime, chop finely the stalks and a little bacon fat and fry this in the pan from which you have just taken the partly-cooked caps. Put this mince over the mushrooms in the baking-dish, moisten with a glassful of wine; season with pepper and salt and the juice of a lemon; cook in a slow oven for about half an hour and serve in the baking-dish.

BROILED MUSHROOMS
: Choose some fairly large, fully-opened mushrooms; clean them and peel them; then soak them in a *marinade* of olive oil or oiled butter for about half an hour. Brush the grill with the same oil or butter and put the mushrooms on the hot grill, stems and gills up; broil quickly, basting them with the oil or butter of the *marinade*. Serve very hot, with a dusting of salt and freshly-ground black pepper.

CASSEROLE MUSHROOMS
: Pick, clean, peel and stem some fairly large and well-opened mushrooms. Put each cap upon a round piece of buttered bread, lining the bottom of a

shallow casserole; season with pepper and salt and put a pat of butter on each mushroom; moisten with a cupful of fresh cream and put the casserole under a grill for 25 minutes, basting with the cream from time to time. Serve hot in the casserole.

CREAMED MUSHROOMS

Clean, trim and stem some small mushrooms and simmer them for 10 to 15 minutes in some rich *velouté*, or in a light cream sauce; season with pepper and salt. Have as many rasped French rolls as there are guests; scoop out of the rolls all the crumb, or as much as possible and put the hollowed rolls in the oven until they are hot and crisp; fill them up then with the creamed mushrooms and pour in and over the rest of the *velouté* or cream sauce in which the mushrooms were cooked.

DEVILLED MUSHROOMS

Fresh mushrooms	Butter
Salt and pepper	Lemon juice
2 hard-boiled eggs	2 raw eggs
Mustard	Cayenne

Peel and wash mushrooms, *sauté* until tender in a sufficiency of butter; then cut into small pieces, seasoning rather highly with salt, pepper and cayenne. Add lemon juice and mustard to taste. Mash the yolks of the hard-boiled eggs, chop the whites finely. Blend to a rough paste with the yolks of raw eggs and heat gently in a small pan, taking care mixture does not boil. Pile on fried *croûtes* or on hot buttered toast decorating with hard-boiled eggs.

CHAMPIGNONS FLAMBES (FOR 4)

Sauté a pound of mushroom caps in butter with plenty of salt in a chafing dish. Pour a cupful of Sherry over them. Simmer until dryish. Then add a small amount of Brandy and light it. When the flame has gone out, add cream to taste.

DALE WARREN

FRIED MUSHROOMS

Pick, clean, trim and peel some medium-sized mushrooms. Melt some butter in a frying-pan and fry the mushrooms in it for about 10 minutes; season with pepper and salt. Take the mushrooms out of the pan and keep them hot in the oven whilst you fry in the butter in the pan some small rounds of bread upon which to serve the mushrooms.

MUSHROOMS AU GRATIN Pick, clean, trim, peel and stem some mushrooms; place them, gills up, in a well-buttered baking-dish and sprinkle over them fresh white breadcrumbs, a little minced parsley and chives, and either a little Parmesan cheese or some finely-chopped ham; season with pepper and salt and pour over it all some liquified butter, then bake for 15 or 20 minutes according to heat.

GRILLED MUSHROOMS Choose some rather large mushrooms, wash them and peel them; cut off the stalks to within $\frac{1}{2}$ in. of caps. Let them stand for an hour in warm, melted butter, turning them over from time to time; season with salt and pepper. Then cook over or under a clear and fierce heat, turning once only. Serve on buttered toast with a squeeze of lemon and a sprinkling of chopped parsley. Bacon fat may be used with advantage in place of butter.

MUSHROOMS SUR LE PLAT Pick, wash, trim and peel some small mushrooms and put them in a fire-proof soup plate or egg dish; put a pat of butter on each mushroom and just a little water in the plate; put a strip of any sort of ordinary paste round the edge of the plate or dish, then reverse another plate or dish, exactly of the same size, press the paste over it all round so that no steam can escape and bake in a moderate oven for 25 minutes. Then remove the top plate and the paste round the edges, wipe the rim of the under plate and serve the mushrooms straight from it.

MUSHROOM PUREE Pick, wash and trim the mushrooms, but do not peel them; dry them carefully, then chop them finely, caps and stems alike. Cook them slowly in hot butter—they must not be *fried* but stewed in butter till soft; they are then seasoned with pepper and salt and a squeeze of lemon, mashed and reheated with more or less *Béchamel Sauce*, according to taste, or some breadcrumbs soaked in gravy, the whole being thoroughly well mixed together before use as a filling of puff paste *darioles*, scooped out tomatoes, egg-plant, baby vegetable marrow, and many other vegetables; or else served as a garnish with cutlets or many other meat, game or fish dishes.

STEWED MUSHROOMS

All kinds of mushrooms, large or small, may be stewed in a number of different ways, but always very gently and never for very long. Butter is the usual fat in which mushrooms are stewed, but bacon fat will do just as well, if not better. Mushrooms may also be stewed in meat stock, in milk and cream, in red or white wine, always being seasoned with a little salt, pepper (the freshly-ground black pepper for choice), a squeeze of lemon juice, and, according to taste, coralline pepper, cayenne or paprika.

SOME MUSHROOM SAUCES, STUFFINGS & GARNITURES

SAUCE CHASSEUR Scald the mushrooms; chop caps and stalks; toss in hot butter or olive oil (or half of each) until tender; season with salt, pepper and a spoonful of finely chopped shallots; remove from the pan and keep warm. Add to the hot butter in the pan a spoonful of flour; stir and cook; add in equal quantities some white wine, stock and tomato purée; simmer until reduced by half or more; add the cooked mushrooms and taste; add whatever seasoning (pepper, salt or a squeeze of lemon) according to taste.

DUXELLES This is the culinary name of a Mushroom preserve used to give a mushroom flavour to sauces, stuffings and various garnishings. It is made usually with the discarded peelings and stalks of fresh mushrooms chopped up finely and cooked in butter with some finely chopped onion and shallots, well seasoned with pepper, salt and a little grated nutmeg. When cold, the mixture is kept in a glass jar covered with buttered paper, ready for use. *Duxelles* sauce is a white wine sauce flavoured with *Duxelles*.

SAUCE FINANCIERE
1 cup brown sauce   Truffle trimmings
$\frac{1}{2}$ cup chicken broth   4 or 5 mushrooms
$\frac{1}{2}$ glass Sauternes or Madeira
Seasonings as desired

Heat the brown sauce, add the chicken broth, the truffles and the chopped mushrooms. Cook over a good heat until liquid is greatly reduced, then add the wine, a little at a time, after reducing the heat. Strain and serve hot.

KETCHUP OR CATSUP A typically English 'bottled sauce.' It is made with sliced fresh mushrooms, seasoned with salt and pepper, and left to soak for five or six days in vinegar flavoured with various spices. The mushrooms are then pressed hard in order to get all their juice and flavour in the liquor in which they have been marinated; this liquor is then boiled, seasoned with pepper, thyme, bayleaf and marjoram; when it is cold, it is filtered and bottled for later use.

SAUCE MADERE

One of the best wine sauces. It is made like a *Sauce Piquante* (minus the pickles and vinegar) in which white wine takes the place of cold water. Add to the strained sauce $\frac{1}{4}$ lb. thinly-sliced fresh mushrooms and the gravy from whatever roast this sauce is to grace, after removing fat from surface. Finally, five minutes before serving, add a wineglassful of good Madeira wine and allow sauce to simmer gently. On festive occasions, sliced or chopped fresh truffles are also added.

GARNITURE MILANAISE

A classical *Garniture* used chiefly for *Escalopes de Veau*. It consists of spaghetti to which is added a *Julienne* of tongue, mushrooms and truffles; also a little tomato sauce, and, just before serving, a light dusting of grated cheese with a pat of fresh butter to each serving.

MUSHROOM SAUCE (OLD STYLE)

"If you wish to make a white *purée* of mushrooms, you must then turn the mushrooms white in a little water and lemon juice; chop them; then put them into a stew-pan, with a very small bit of butter. When the mushrooms are what we call melted, moisten them with four or six spoonfuls of *velouté*. Do not let them boil long, for fear they should lose their taste and colour. Then rub them through a tammy. It is no easy matter, indeed, with regard to mushrooms, yet this sauce is called *purée* of mushrooms.

It is almost useless to observe, that for the brown *purée*, it is enough to moisten with some *Espagnole* only. If you were to fry the mushrooms brown, they then would turn black, and make the sauce of the like colour. Skim your sauce. Put a little sugar into both. All such sauces as are called *purée*, must be made thicker than others."

LOUIS EUSTACHE UDE: *The French Cook*, 1814

MUSHROOM SAUCE (NEW STYLE) Add fresh and thinly-sliced mushrooms to a *Béchamel* (q.v.). Cook gently in a double-boiler for about 30 minutes. Some cooks believe in the slice mushrooms being lightly *sautés* before adding to the sauce, straining into it also the butter they have been cooked in.

MUSHROOM SAUCE FOR OYSTERS (AMERICAN)

2½ tablespoons butter
3 medium-sized mushrooms
1½ teaspoons flour
½ cup thin cream
¼ teaspoon chopped parsley
1 tablespoon grated cheese
3 shallots
1 egg yolk
Salt and cayenne

This is the sauce usually served with baked oysters. Melt half the quantity of butter in a pan, add the chopped shallots and finely chopped mushrooms, cooking all together gently for 15 minutes. Meantime, melt remainder of butter, add flour and, when mixture begins to bubble, moisten gradually with the cream. Stir until sauce is smooth and thick. Beat the egg yolk, add the sauce slowly to it, mixing well; then add the shallots and mushrooms and their butter. Season rather highly with cayenne and salt and sprinkle in some parsley.

PROVENCALE SAUCE

3 tablespoons pure olive oil
3 shallots
¼ lb. mushrooms
Good stock or bouillon
1 small glass white wine
1 small 'bouquet-garni'
1 small clove of garlic
1 dessertspoon flour
Salt and pepper
Lemon juice to taste

Chop together, rather finely, shallots and garlic and, after having heated some oil, lightly brown them, stirring frequently. Sprinkle with flour, moisten with meat stock or *bouillon*, season with salt and pepper; add white wine and *bouquet* and cover closely. Let it simmer gently for 15 minutes, then add the chopped mushrooms, and let it simmer for 20 or 30 minutes more. Strain, add lemon juice and serve with, for instance, cold roast beef or veal.

SAUCES REGENCE There are two *Sauces Régence*, one for fish and the other for chicken: the first is a *Sauce Normande*, with white wine, mushrooms and truffles added; the other a *Sauce Suprême*, also with white wine, mushrooms and truffles added. Both the *Sauce Normande* and the *Sauce Suprême* are *Veloutés*, the first with a *fumet* of soles and some *essence* of mushrooms added; the second with some fresh cream added at the last moment before serving.

MUSHROOM STUFFING

6 oz. fresh mushrooms
6 oz. fresh breadcrumbs
1 oz. butter
1 small rasher bacon
Salt, pepper, nutmeg
1 egg

Wash and dry mushrooms, using stalks if firm and white. Chop them rather finely. Cut up the rasher of bacon and fry lightly with the mushrooms, stirring all the time. Add this to the breadcrumbs and season well. Bind mixture with the butter and the ingredients, including the bits of fried salt pork. Nice for duck, goose or with roast pork.

MUSHROOM STUFFING

Mince as finely as possible on a board the same weight of parsley and trimmed mushrooms; mince also a little less than half the weight of shallots and cook it all in hot butter on a brisk heat for five minutes; season to taste and stir with a wooden spoon. Sometimes breadcrumbs and a beaten egg are added to the mixture to give it gerater consistency, and when this stuffing is used for filling boned pigeons, larks or quails, the bird's liver is also added to the stuffing.

VICTORIA SAUCE

This is a *Sauce Allemande* (q.v.) to which some good white wine has been added in the proportion of one measure of white wine to three of sauce; the two are thoroughly warmed up together with some chopped cooked mushrooms added, without being allowed to boil. In the meantime, some lobster coral is pounded with some fresh butter, and, when the two are thoroughly well mixed, they are added to the sauce and stirred until it is time to serve.

SOME BASIC SAUCES USED FOR MUSHROOM RECIPES

ALLEMANDE One of the classic French sauces, also known as *Sauce Blonde* and *Sauce Parisienne*. To make a *Sauce Allemande*, one requires:

2 cupfuls of *Sauce Velouté* (q.v.)   2 egg-yolks
Fresh butter or thick cream   A little nutmeg

Reduce the *Velouté* upon a slow fire until it is but half the original quantity. Pour into a double-boiler, or, failing this, in a small saucepan which must be set in another larger pan containing hot water. Beat two egg-yolks and add to sauce, stirring gently during addition. Next, add cream or butter sufficient to enrich and improve the flavour of the sauce; also a light dusting of nutmeg, some essence of mushrooms, or lemon juice to taste. Cook in or over gently boiling water, stirring frequently until the sauce is thick and very creamy.

BEARNAISE One of the most popular sauces for a fillet of beef, or most grilled red meats. It is not peculiar to Béarn, but was named by the chef of the Pavillon Henry IV, at St. Germain, near Paris, who first introduced this sauce, in 1835.

1 or 2 shallots   Sprig fresh tarragon
2 or 3 stalks chervil   2 tablespoons wine
4 egg yolks   Salt and pepper
Half a pound best fresh butter
2 tablespoons cold water

Chop shallots, tarragon leaves and chervil *very* finely. Place in a small saucepan, add white wine and allow the lot to simmer very gently until the wine has almost entirely evaporated; then add cold water. Strain and set aside. Place the egg yolks in the upper part of a double boiler, add the prepared herb and wine mixture and gently whisk with a wire whip, adding the butter one piece at a time, beating until

22

absorbed before adding another piece. The beating must not be too fast; it must be steady and continuous over the *almost* boiling water until the sauce is as thick as Mayonnaise. Should the sauce curdle or *separate*, remove pan from fire, add a small teaspoonful of cold water and whip rather vigorously until sauce is thick and very smooth. Serve hot, either spread with a sprinkling of chopped chervil and tarragon on grilled meat or separately in a sauce-boat.

BECHAMEL

The name of one of the basic French sauces and one of the creamiest white sauces. It was named after, and believed to have been introduced by, Louis de Béchameil, or Béchamel, Marquis de Nointel, Lord Steward of the Household at the Court of Louis XIV.

The flour and water, sticky and lumpy horror so often served under this name, is a libellous imitation, but it is not a *Béchamel*. To make a *Béchamel* in the old-fasioned and best manner, one should use butter and flour in equal quantities and the best and creamiest milk, as follows:

Melt the butter, but do not allow to sizzle, in a small saucepan over a rather low heat. When the butter is melted, add the flour, stirring well into the butter. Have some cold boiled milk. When the butter and flour mixture begins to bubble gently, add the cold milk, very little at a time, stirring and beating well until the whole amount of milk has been added and the sauce is thick and creamy. This is the *Sauce Béchamel*. It may be used as a basis for other sauces by adding anything called for by the recipe chosen: mushrooms, chopped parsley, chopped hard-boiled egg, oysters, or whatnot. If to be served plain, and if a rich sauce be required, add the beaten yolk of an egg—after removing the pan from the fire—and a little lemon juice.

ESPAGNOLE OR BROWN SAUCE

One of the three *Grandes Sauces—Velouté* and *Béchamel* being the other two—or basic sauces from which most others are made. Here is a classical recipe for making *Sauce Espagnole*:

Trimmings of raw veal and ham or game
1 onion and 1 carrot   2 dessertspoons flour
1 whole clove   Hot stock or *bouillon*
1 small *'bouquet-garni'* Salt and pepper

The meat trimmings must be lean, veal and ham for choice, but, if more convenient, scraps of rabbit, pork or game will do. Have a heavy iron pan and in this place the pieces of meat, an onion (cut up), a whole clove and a carrot cut into slices. The heat should be gentle and the pan closely covered. Cook slowly until a rich brown gravy be obtained; then sprinkle in a dessertspoonful of flour, stirring so as to work it into all ingredients until lightly browned. Moisten with some hot stock or *bouillon* and add salt, pepper and a *"bouquet-garni"*. Cook gently over very little heat or on the far edge of the stove for four hours. The sauce should be of the consistency of thick cream. When done, skim to remove surface fat, if any, and strain through a fine wire sieve. This sauce may be kept in a cool place for some time and may be used as a basis for other sauces. Mention will be made in other sections of this book of the various uses to which this sauce may be put.

MORNAY This is a 'cheesed' *Sauce Béchamel* (q.v.) in a double boiler. The desired quantity of grated Parmesan cheese is stirred in the *Sauce*, and a little Cayenne pepper may also be added before serving. If used with fish, add essence of fish.

PIQUANTE

2 oz. butter $1\frac{1}{2}$ oz. flour
4 oz. chopped onions Salt and pepper
One or two vinegar pickles White wine

Gently melt the butter in a copper (or earthenware) saucepan until it begins to smoke slightly, then throw in the onions and stir, cooking them until they are a rather dark, even, golden colour. Now add the flour, stirring until the entire mixture is an even brown. Moisten with white wine, adding it little by little and stirring well all the time. The sauce should be of the consistency of a thick white sauce. Season to taste and allow to simmer over a low heat for 15 to 20 minutes. The sauce may be passed through a *chinois* (which is a conical metal sieve) or not, as preferred. Cut up one or two vinegar gherkins, add them to the sauce, with chopped parsley, chervil and tarragon, and simmer for five or ten minutes longer. The gravy from whatever meat is intended to be served with this sauce, should be added to it; failing this, add a little good meat essence. When adding the gravy, skim off fat first or the sauce will be too rich. Some cooks also add a little French mustard; this is entirely a matter of taste.

POULETTE

A variant of the *Sauce Béchamel*.

    2 tablespoons butter   2 tablespoons flour
    2 cups bouillon or stock   Salt and pepper
    1 very small 'bouquet'   Lemon juice to taste
    2 tablespoons thick cream   1 or 2 egg yolks

Make in the same way as white or cream sauce, taking care the flour does not colour. Moisten with any good white stock or use the liquid of the meat to be served with this sauce. When the sauce is smooth and thick, remove from heat, beat in cream, and egg yolks, seasonings.

ROUX

A generic term for various flour bindings. A *roux* is sometimes brown, sometimes white or *blond*, according to the use that it is intended for. It is really but a *Béchamel* sauce (q.v.) in its essentials. One or more spoonfuls of butter are placed in a small saucepan and, when it is melted, the same amount of flour is added and stirred into the butter. If a 'thin' sauce is required, one spoonful of flour is used to two of butter. The mixture must colour gently to the desired shade, then the liquid indicated by the recipe is added, little by little, and the sauce seasoned as desired and allowed to mellow by the side of the stove. The dripping from a piece of roast meat is sometimes used instead of butter; this improves the flavour of the sauce if intended to be served with the roast.

VELOUTE

    2 tablespoons of butter   2 medium-sized onions
    A *bouquet-garni*   A slice or scraps of ham
    Scraps of white meat, raw and lean
    2 carrots   A few mushrooms
    1 pint or more water   1 or 2 cloves
    Salt and pepper   1 cup white sauce
    More cold water

The above ingredients are sufficient for a small household. If a large quantity of this basic sauce is needed to be kept on hand, a small fowl must be added.

Melt the butter in a heavy saucepan, add the sliced carrots and onions, then the pieces or slice of lean ham and the scraps of lean meat, also the *bouquet-garni*. A small boiling fowl is also helpful. All this must gently 'sweat' over a low fire, but the ingredients must *not* colour. To prevent this, add a pint of water as soon as colouring is likely to begin and continue gently cooking until the gravy is greatly reduced. If a fowl is in the pan, it must, at this juncture, be stuck all over with a fork to let the juices flow into the gravy. Now fill the pan with cold water, after adding the salt, pepper to taste, a few fresh, peeled mushrooms, if available, and the cloves. Cover closely and cook gently for four hours, after skimming carefully just as the contents of the pan start boiling. Strain, when done, through a fine sieve and pour stock into another saucepan. Bring contents to boiling point, then gently stir in the white sauce, stirring constantly until blended with the stock. This sauce may also be kept in the ice-box for some time, if required, in sufficient quantities to warrant making a large amount. When the white sauce has been added, the mixture should gently simmer over a low heat, to improve the flavour, before cooling, to store.

MUSHROOMS FOR BREAKFAST

BACON AND EGGS are old and tried friends always welcome at breakfast time: unfortunately we do not see nearly enough of them since the war. Mushrooms, happily, are not rationed, and we are still at liberty to have all the mushrooms we want. Mushrooms, either grilled or stewed, make an excellent main dish for breakfast by themselves, but they are even more admirable when partnered with bacon, ham, kidneys or eggs, or whatever happens to be in the larder of a morning. They are particularly helpful with scrambled eggs that came out of a cardboard packet in powder form, as these are sometimes somewhat unpleasantly 'eggy' by themselves. But mushrooms will also partner very well indeed the boiled potatoes of the night before which have been tossed and browned in fat for breakfast; they also taste good with grilled or fried tomatoes. Try them in any way you fancy any day, and you will soon find out that you cannot do better than 'Mushrooms for breakfast.'

SCRAMBLED EGGS WITH MUSHROOMS

Cook sliced mushrooms in butter gently for a few minutes. Drain, cool and add to beaten eggs, using the butter the mushrooms were cooked in for scrambling the eggs.

MUSHROOMS FOR LUNCHEON

MUSHROOMS may be served at luncheon time in many different ways, as hors d'oeuvre, cold or hot, as an Entrée, or at the end of the meal. But they are also most welcome with fish, meat, poultry and game light dishes, which they make more nourishing as well as more flavoursome and toothsome. Here are a few suggestions how to serve mushrooms at lunch time either by themselves or as part of various recipes.

SALADE DE CHAMPIGNONS (HORS D'ŒUVRE) Pick, trim, wash, peel and stem some fairly large mushrooms. Dry them well and slice them in very thin slices. Cook these gently in hot butter—stew but do not fry—for a few minutes only, so that they are still firm, although not hard. Let them get quite cold and serve with a dressing of olive oil, lemon juice and freshly-ground black pepper.

BANQUETTES OF MUSHROOMS Small oval pastry 'boats' which are baked and allowed to get cold before being filled with chopped-up mushrooms cooked for about 15 minutes in a *Velouté*, which is then poured over them.

BOUCHEES AUX CHAMPIGNONS Small puff-paste cases filled with diced or sliced mushrooms with either a brown or a white sauce.

CANAPES PAULINE

Uncooked chicken livers 1 small chopped onion
Butter Salt and cayenne
Finely chopped lean ham Brown Sauce
Rounds of bread Parsley
Chopped white of hard-boiled egg
Yolk of 1 or 2 hard-boiled eggs
Chopped fresh mushrooms

Chop the raw chicken livers very finely, after removing nerves. Fry them in a little butter with a small quantity of onion and, when beginning to brown, add half as much finely-mir   as there was chicken liver mixture, add also one or two chopped mushrooms. Cook all this gently together and bind to a paste with brown sauce, seasoning to taste with salt and Cayenne. Spread this mixture thickly on rounds of toasted or sauté bread and sift hard-boiled egg yolk over surface, placing in the centre of each round thus prepared a circle of chopped egg white and a tiny sprig of parsley. It is impossible to give definite quantities of ingredients as they depend on the number of canapés being made.

CHAMPIGNONS AU BEURRE

Wash and peel some fairly large mushrooms; cut them up in three or four thick slices, according to size; season them with pepper and salt; toss them in sizzling butter in an open pan until tender and serve straight away whilst hot.

CHAMPIGNONS BOURGEOISE

Pick, wipe, trim and cut in half the required number of mushrooms. Put some slices of streaky bacon into a stewpan and cook them over a slow fire for 15 minutes; then add the mushrooms, some minced chives and a little finely-chopped parsley; season with pepper and salt; moisten with some dry white wine, dredge with a little flour, and stew very gently until the sauce is quite thick; the mushrooms and the sauce should then be served on squares of fried bread.

CHAMPIGNONS AUX FINES HERBES

The same as *Champignons au beurre*, but with some finely chopped parsley added at the last moment.

CHAMPIGNONS A LA GRECQUE

Small mushrooms left to marinade in olive oil and lemon juice overnight, then cooked in the marinade, allowed to get cold and served as a cold hors d'oeuvre with a little lemon juice added at the last moment.

CHAMPIGNONS A LA HONGROISE

Small mushrooms washed, peeled and cut in halves; well seasoned with pepper and salt and a little paprika; cooked in butter for a few minutes only, then cover with hot cream or a rich hot white sauce and finish cooking in it. Serve very hot.

CHAMPIGNONS A LA LYONNAISE

The same as *Champignons au beurre* with some onion finely chopped and cooked in butter added to them.

CHAMPIGNONS MARINES	Small mushrooms marinaded in vinegar, bay leaf and onion, then cooked in it and allowed to get quite cold before being served as a *hors d'oeuvre*.
CHAMPIGNONS A LA POULETTE	Large mushrooms cut in four or five pieces, according to size, seasoned and cooked in butter; then served covered with a *sauce poulette* and a dusting of finely chopped parsley.
FLAN AUX CHAMPIGNONS	Evenly sliced mushrooms which, after being cooked in butter, are neatly arranged in straight rows on a base of Tart pastry, usually rather long and narrow. The mushrooms are then lightly covered with a rich *Velouté* (q.v.), seasoned with pepper and salt and a little lemon juice (sometimes also a dusting of grated cheese), then made very hot under a not too fierce grill.
OMELETTE AUX CHAMPIGNONS	Pick, wash, trim, peel some mushrooms and chop them up, caps and stems; toss them in hot butter till done, season to taste and fold them in an omelette just before serving.
OMELETTE AUX CHAMPIGNONS (NORMANDE)	Shelled shrimps and shredded mushrooms folded in; garnish with poached oysters, truffles and *Sauce Normande*.
NOODLES WITH MUSHROOMS	Wash but do not peel the required quantity of mushrooms; cut them up and put them in a saucepan with just a little stock or milk; simmer gently for 10 to 15 minutes; add a few breadcrumbs, and stir smartly until all the moisture has gone. Add butter; also salt and pepper to taste; rub through a fine strainer and keep the purée of mushrooms warm on the side of the stove until wanted. When the noodles have been cooked, moisten the purée of mushrooms with cream or milk and pour it over the noodles in the serving dish. A dusting of grated cheese and a final browning under the grill is a welcome *variante*.
ŒUFS AU PLAT AND ŒUFS AU FOUR	These are fried eggs and baked eggs, and there are many ways, in the *Cuisine Classique*, of preparing them with mushrooms, such as:

Fried eggs served with shredded mushrooms, sheep's kidneys and horseradish; also half a fried tomato per egg. **COLETTE**

Heat some butter in a pan, and when it begins to brown, mince in it a shallot and 2 small onions. Reduce heat and add 2 or 3 chopped mushrooms and a little minced ham; also salt and pepper. Then add as much white wine as may be necessary to work the whole into a smooth paste, mixing well over the fire all the whole but not letting it boil; when ready to use, add a little chopped parsley and then cover the bottom of small china fireproof dishes with this mixture, having previously buttered them well. Break carefully two eggs in each dish over the mushroom or *duxelle* lining; then bake in a hot oven for 5 minutes. **DUXELLES**

Fried eggs served upon a slice of ham and with a garnish of small fried mushrooms. **ERMENONVILLE**

Fried eggs served with mushrooms and horseradish. **PETIT-DUC**

Fried eggs served with some lamb sweetbread, truffles and a little fresh cream. **SAINT-HONORE**

The bones are removed. To the flesh of the eels is added a stuffing made of buttered whiting and minced mushrooms, the whole being braised in a terrine with chopped shallots, white Pouilly wine, a little brandy, butter, mushrooms and a few onions lightly browned beforehand. **ANGUILLES BEAUCAIRE**

		MACKEREL A L'ITALIENNE
1 large or two medium fish	2 small onions	
White wine court-bouillon	Salt and pepper	
2 tablespoons olive oil	1 bayleaf	
1 small clove garlic	White wine	
2 large fresh mushrooms	Chopped parsley	

Half-cook the cleaned fish in the *court-bouillon*. Brown the chopped onions, mushrooms, garlic and parsley in olive oil, then moisten with wine and season as wished. Add the mackerel, well drained and not too much done, and the bayleaf. Simmer very gently until the fish is sufficiently cooked; then serve, covering with its own strained liquor.

MATELOTE A fish stew, usually rather rich, made with red wine, sometimes with white wine or cider, and eel, herrings, bream and other types of fish. Here is the classical *Matelote* recipe:

2 large onions	Flour
2 tablespoons butter	1 bottle red wine
½ lb. fresh mushrooms	½ lb. small onions
Pepper	Sundry spices
About 2 lb. skinned and cut-up eel or other fish	

Cut up the large onions and, as soon as the butter begins to smoke slightly, put them in to fry. When golden brown, add the flour to onions, stirring well, then moisten with the red wine (Burgundy for choice). Add the small onions and the sliced mushrooms as well as such spices as are customary: one clove, dusting of nutmeg, pinch of ginger, pepper (not too much) and a small pinch of cinnamon. Cover closely and cook this sauce gently for nearly an hour, then add the pieces of eel and cook for a quarter of an hour. Decorate the dish with small fried *croûtons* and, on special occasions, add, before serving, a small glassful of brandy which has been previously set alight. Add this just one minute before serving.

BAKED STUFFED SMELTS

6 smelts	3 or 4 mushrooms
5 or 6 oysters	A small onion
½ teaspoon chopped parsely	Lemon juice
Salt and pepper	1 tablespoon butter
1 tablespoon thick cream	Buttered crumbs

Clean and wipe fish dry. Peel and *sauté* the mushrooms. Parboil, then drain and chop oysters. Mix together finely chopped parsley, onion, salt, pepper, chopped mushrooms, oyster and cream. Use this mixture to stuff smelts. Lay them in an oven dish, sprinkle with salt and pepper and brush over with lemon juice. Cover with a buttered paper and bake for five minutes in a hot oven, then remove paper and sprinkle with buttered breadcrumbs and continue baking until these are brown and fish is done. Serve with a good Béarnaise Sauce.

BROCHETTES OF KIDNEYS

Lamb or sheep's kidneys
Thick rashers mild bacon
Salt and pepper
Mushrooms
Butter

Skin, core and cut up kidneys into chunky pieces. Cut the bacon into pieces of similar size and thickness. Peel and wash mushrooms, cut them also into similar sized pieces and lightly *sauté* them in butter, seasoning with salt and pepper. Retain the butter they are cooked in for other uses. Allow mushrooms to cool and do not cook too much. Now thread on special skewers first a piece of kidney, next a piece of bacon and thirdly a piece of mushroom, continuing until skewer is full. Cook under the grill, lightly dusting with salt and pepper. Serve very hot, on skewers, either on toast or *croûtons*.

ROGNONS A LA BERICHONNE

Sheep's kidneys
Fried croûtons
Salt pork
Tiny 'button' onions
Butter
Red wine
Fresh mushrooms
Salt and pepper

Skin and cut kidneys in halves. *Sauté* them in butter and place each half on a hot *croûton* of same size. Pour half a glass of red wine into the pan the kidneys were cooked in, stirring well; season and cook rapidly until reduced to half original volume, then add a 'nut' of butter and, if available, a spoonful of good meat extract or glaze. Cover kidneys with this gravy and serve them around a small ragoût composed of fried cubes of salt pork, sauté mushroom caps and glazed onions.

FRICASSEE DE POULET

1 chicken
1 tablespoon flour
Salt and pepper
Small pinch grated nutmeg
1 teaspoon lemon juice
12 or 15 small onions
2 tablespoons butter
1 cup water or stock
1 or 2 stalks parsley
3 egg yolks
$\frac{1}{2}$ lb. fresh mushrooms
Fried croûtons

After having prepared the chicken for cooking, cut into neat pieces and allow these to stand for half an hour in tepid water, to whiten the flesh. Drain well and dry with a cloth. Heat the butter, add the flour, stirring until the mixture is smooth, moisten with the water or stock (some people prefer a mixture of water and white wine). Season with salt, pepper and nutmeg, add the parsley and, if available, some chives. Add the pieces of chicken, cover closely and simmer gently for an hour and a half or until the chicken is quite tender. Remove pan from fire and add beaten egg yolks and the lemon juice. The mushrooms and the small onions must be added when the chicken has been simmering for nearly an hour. Serve with croûtons as garnish, alternating with the small onions and the mushroom caps. Sprinkle with a little minced parsley.

FRIED CHICKEN TARTARE

1 or 2 small spring chickens
Chopped fresh mushrooms
Chopped parsley
1 clove minced garlic
Fine brown breadcrumbs
Ice-cold tartare sauce
Salt and pepper
Butter
Frying fat
Chopped chives

Split the chickens down the back and clean interior well. Break the bones and soak in hot melted butter to which the chopped garlic and herbs have been added, as well as salt and pepper and the finely-chopped mushrooms. Cover and allow to marinate, turning occasionally for a couple of hours. Now drain halves of chicken, dip each in melted butter and coat evenly with the breadcrumbs, pressing them firmly on. Fry in an open pan or grill over a low heat, turning to cook evenly. Serve very hot with the sauce Tartare handed separately. In order to allow the pieces of chicken to marinate nicely, keep the mixture near the stove so that the butter remains liquid.

PLANKED BROILER

$\frac{1}{4}$ tablespoon green pepper
$\frac{1}{4}$ tablespoon red pepper
1 teaspoon minced onion
$\frac{1}{4}$ tablespoon chopped parsley
1 teaspoon lemon juice
1 spring chicken, split
Hot, freshly-mashed potatoes
Sauté mushroom caps
$\frac{1}{2}$ clove minced garlic
$\frac{1}{4}$ cup butter
Salt
Extra butter

A special seasoned 'plank' is required for this. Beat

the butter to a cream, add to it the peppers, the onion, garlic, parsley and lemon juice. Put the chicken in a baking-tin, skin side down. Sprinkle with salt and pepper, dot over with small pieces of butter and bake in a hot oven for 15 to 20 minutes or until nearly done, basting twice with hot butter when cooking. Brush the plank over with melted butter, pipe a border of the mashed potatoes around the extreme edge of the plank, place chicken in centre, breast side upwards, and spread it with the butter mixture. Add the mushrooms, previously cooked in butter, and place the whole thing in a very hot oven to brown the potatoes evenly. Slip the plank on a platter to serve. If wished, the broiler may be jointed into serving portions before sending to the table, and sprigs of watercress may be used as a decoration.

CROQUETTES OF CHICKEN

2 tablespoons flour
$\frac{1}{2}$ lb. cold cooked chicken
Lemon juice to taste
$\frac{1}{4}$ lb. small mushrooms
Fine brown breadcrumbs
1 tablespoon thick cream
1 small truffle (optional)
Frying oil or fat

$\frac{1}{2}$ cup stock
Butter
Salt and pepper
2 oz. boiled ham
1 egg

The perfect chicken croquette is a delicious dish: the interior should not be too firm and the creamy substance must contrast with the crisp exterior.

Chop or mince the chicken finely with the ham. Toss the mushrooms, after chopping them, in a sufficiency of butter. Chop the truffle, if any. Blend all ingredients, add salt, pepper and a touch of Cayenne, if liked. Melt a couple of tablespoons of butter without allowing it to brown, add flour and moisten with stock, beating to a smooth sauce which should be quite thick. Add the chicken mixture to this, with the cream. Cool mixture, then shape as desired into croquettes or 'corks,' dip carefully first in the beaten egg, then in breadcrumbs; allow this to harden a little, then fry until a nice light brown in oil or fat at 475°F. if a thermometer is used, if not, in slightly smoking fat. Serve at once with any desired sauce handed separately.

COMPOTE OF PIGEONS

2 plump young pigeons
1 teaspoon flour
½ cup white wine
¼ lb. fresh mushrooms
Fat bacon or salt pork
½ cup hot water

1 small *bouquet-garni*
Butter
Small white onions
Pinch sugar
Salt and pepper
Tiny dusting nutmeg

Truss pigeons. Cut into small pieces a slice of either fat pork or bacon and cook gently to extract fat, removing pieces left over after the completion of that operation. Brown the pigeons in this fat on all sides and lightly dust with salt. When a nice even colour on all sides, add to the birds another rather thick slice of streaky bacon, cut into dice, and continue browning gently with the pigeons, taking care they do not colour unevenly. Dust with the flour, then add the hot water and the white wine. Boil up sharply for 5 or 6 minutes, then add *bouquet*, salt and pepper to taste, and greatly reduce heat or pull pan to edge of stove to finish cooking the pigeons. They must be closely covered during the cooking. Meanwhile, brown as many tiny onions as you may wish to use in a sufficiency of butter, adding a tiny pinch of powdered sugar. When the birds are half done, add these browned onions and, 20 minutes later, the mushrooms, slicing if large but use preferably the tiny 'button' mushrooms if available. Cook for 10 minutes longer. Drain the pigeons and keep hot after removing strings. Make the gravy in the usual way and serve the birds very hot, surrounded by the mushrooms and onions, straining the gravy over them and decorating with either watercress tips or parsley.

TURKEY GIBLETS BOURGEOISE

1 set turkey giblets
1 *bouquet-garni*
2 cloves
2 tablespoons butter
3 or 4 fresh mushrooms
1 pinch or small sprig basil

Salt and pepper
2 tablespoons flour
1 clove garlic
Young white turnips
2 cups good bouillon

Clean thoroughly wing tips, feet, neck, liver and gizzard of a turkey. Brown all this in the heated butter and sprinkle with the flour. Moisten with the *bouillon,* season with salt and freshly ground pepper and add the cut-up mushrooms and other ingredients. Cover and cook until all is tender. Brown some small young turnips in butter and add to giblet stew when half-cooked. Remove any excess fat and serve with 'short' sauce.

LANCASHIRE HOT-POT

2 lb. neck of mutton
3 sheeps' kidneys
½ lb. fresh mushrooms
12 oysters
2 lb. potatoes
3 onions
2 oz. butter

Remove all excess of fat and cut the meat into cutlets. Peel the potatoes and cut them up in thick slices. Peel the onions and cut in thin slices. Wash but do not peel the mushrooms and cut them in two. Skin and halve the kidneys, removing core. Put all ingredients in a deep pan in alternate layers, with a layer of potatoes on top and seasoning each layer with pepper and salt. Melt the butter and pour it over; also 2 breakfast cups of meat stock. Cover closely and cook very gently in the oven or on top of stove for $2\frac{1}{2}$ hours. Serve in cooking pot.

MIXED GRILL

A testing dish for the cook, owing to the need to allow the correct frying time to each of the various kinds and sizes of meat which compose it, so that each is done to a turn at the instant of serving. An assortment usual in England is one for each person of a grilled cutlet, sausage, kidney and tomato, served plain but accompanied by choice of bottled sauces, and this may be greatly improved by the addition of mushrooms.

VEAU MARENGO

2 lb. lean breast of veal
½ lb. onions
2 tablespoons flour
3 tablespoons olive oil
1 lb. ripe tomatoes
½ lb. mushrooms
2 cups *bouillon*
Salt and pepper
1 cup dry white wine

Heat the olive oil and brown in it the cut-up meat, then add the chopped onion, browning a little also with meat. Sprinkle with flour, browning that too, then moisten with the mixed wine and bouillon or stock. Season well. Add the sliced mushrooms and the tomatoes, previously reduced to a pulp by slow cooking after peeling. Cover pan closely and allow contents to simmer gently for at least an hour and a half. Some gourmets add one grated clove of garlic.

BLANQUETTE DE VEAU (NEW STYLE) Cut veal in cubes and pour boiling salted water over it and let it soak for 20 minutes. Drain it and put in a pan; cover with water. Add small white onions, salt, pepper, a carrot sliced in quarters, bayleaf, a sprig of parsley. Bring to a boil and simmer slowly. When meat is done, make a white sauce with the stock. Let it cook for 20 minutes. Bind it with 2 yolks of eggs mixed with ½ cup cream. Pour over meat and onions and add mushrooms cooked separately.
MRS. CARROLL CARSTAIRS

BLANQUETTE OF VEAL WITH MUSHROOMS (OLD STYLE) "The veal for this purpose must first be roasted and, when cold, cut into round thin scollops about an inch in diameter; to these add some button-mushrooms also cut into scollops, and enough *Sauce Allemande* (q.v.) for the *entrée*. Just before sending it to table, warm the *blanquette* and dish it up with a border of *croquettes* of veal, of rice or of potatoes."
FRANCATELLI: *The Modern Cook*, 1853

BOUILLI AU GRATIN

Cold bouilli	Butter
Breadcrumbs	Fresh mushrooms
1 onion	1 shallot
Chopped parsley	Bouillon
Tomato purée	Meat glaze or extract

Cut the cold beef into even slices. Melt a sufficiency of butter in an oven-dish; when melted, sprinkle bottom of dish thickly with brown breadcrumbs. Add slices of beef, cover them with sliced mushrooms, the chopped and mixed onion and shallot and parsley, as desired. Moisten with bouillon, tomato purée, and meat glaze, sprinkle surface with more breadcrumbs and brown in oven for 15 minutes.

SALMIS D'AGNEAU

1 or 2 mushrooms	1 cup stock or gravy
2 tablespoons butter	Few stoned olives
Salt and pepper	Chopped parsley
Thin slices cold roast lamb	
½ tablespoon chopped onion	
Sippets of toast or croûtons	

Brown the onion in the butter lightly. Add the lamb, heat through, season with salt and pepper and cover with the stock or, if possible, lamb gravy. Serve up, slices overlapping one another, surrounding with pieces of toast or *croûtons*, the stoned olives and mushroom caps, previously *sauté* in butter.

Slices of cold roast mutton	Hot fried croûtons	**ESCALOPES DE**
1½ cup fresh tomato sauce	Fresh mushrooms	**MOUTON AUX**
Cayenne pepper and salt		**CHAMPIGNONS**

Slice the meat carefully, not too thinly. Boil the peeled mushrooms in salted water, to which a squeeze of lemon juice has been added, until tender. Cut the mushrooms into thin slices. Have some freshly made hot tomato sauce. Season rather highly with cayenne and salt. Add the slices of meat and the mushrooms, just heating both nicely through, but not boiling. Serve with *croûtons* as a garnish, cut into fancy shape.

1 young rabbit	2 tablespoons butter	**LAPIN EN**
Small 'button' onions	1 or 2 egg yolks	**BLANQUETTE**
1 small piece lemon peel	Lemon juice	
1 rather thick slice salt pork	2 tablespoons flour	
1 small '*bouquet-garni*'	Salt and pepper corns	
2 tablespoons cream (optional)		
Small fresh mushrooms (optional)		

This is first-cousin to the homely boiled rabbit, but it will be found to be a far more succulent dish. Cut the rabbit into neat pieces and soak them in cold salted water for a little while to remove excess of blood and so whiten the flesh. When ready, drain and put pieces of rabbit into a heavy stewing-pan, together with salt, a few peppercorns—tied in a piece of muslin—the 'bouquet' and about 12 small onions. Add also a tiny piece of lemon peel, and the salt pork, cut into neat pieces. Barely cover all with cold water and set the pan over a rather low heat, bringing contents slowly to the boil and skimming as required. Keep covered and cook until the rabbit is tender, then remove pieces of meat, keep them hot, strain the broth and also keep hot. Melt the butter in another saucepan, add the flour and stir until mixture is smooth then moisten gradually with the hot rabbit broth, of which there should be about 2 cupfuls. Add the cream, if used, beaten with the egg yolk (or yolks) after the stewing-pan has been removed from the fire. Season to taste with a little lemon juice. If mushrooms are used—and they improve the dish greatly—select small ones and slice French-fashion, that is, cut stems off to within half an inch of caps, peel the mushrooms and the bit of stem, and slice each one from top of cap to bottom of stem, rather thinly. They should be added about ten minutes before the rabbit is done. The pieces of pork, onions and mushrooms are, naturally, served in the creamy sauce, with the rabbit, and light hot mashed potatoes should accompany the dish.

LAPIN CHASSEUR

2 oz. butter	4 onions
2 rabbits	2 sprigs thyme
6 oz. fresh pork	2 bay leaves
3 glasses dry white wine	2 dessertspoonfuls flour
Small cup cream or 2 yolks egg	
1 spoonful chopped parsley	4 to 6 oz. mushrooms

Sauté rabbit pieces in butter until brown, with diced fresh pork, small (or diced) onions, and allow to simmer in casserole with herbs, spices, and white wine until tender (about an hour).

Mushrooms cut up are fried in butter and added to rabbit in casserole. The sauce is finished with addition of cream and yolks of eggs. Sprinkle with chopped parsley before serving.

LE CIVET DE LAPIN

1 rabbit	2 slices bacon (streaky)
½ lb. fresh mushrooms	Blood of rabbit
2 tablespoons flour	2 medium-sized onions
1 thick slice salt pork	1 bottle red Burgundy
Bouquet-garni	Fried *croûtons*
Small pinch ground nutmeg	Salt and pepper

Cut the salt pork and bacon into dice and gently brown in a heavy iron pan (*cocotte*). Remove and set aside lean pieces of pork and bacon and brown cut-up rabbit in the fat in pan, adding the sliced onions. Stir frequently to colour pieces of meat on all sides. Now sprinkle the flour over all, stirring to coat pieces of meat. Allow this to brown a little, then moisten gradually with the wine. Add salt, pepper, *bouquet* and spice (also, if liked, a cut-up clove of garlic), the sliced mushrooms and the small pieces of browned pork and bacon. Cover pan and simmer contents very gently for about an hour and a half. Ten minutes before serving add the blood of the rabbit to thicken and flavour sauce. Remove *bouquet* and serve very hot with hot fried *croûtons*.

SNIPE PUDDING

Six fresh snipe	Cayenne
Lemon juice	1 onion
1 tablespoonful flour	Herbs
Parsley	A suspicion of garlic
Chopped mushrooms	Nutmeg
Suet paste	Truffles
½ pint wine	

Halve the snipe, removing the gizzards and reserving the trail (*for entrail or intestines.* ED.). Season the snipe with cayenne and lemon juice and set aside till required. Slice up the onion, fry a light brown colour, add the mushrooms, parsley, garlic, nutmeg, and herbs; moisten with wine and boil all for 10 minutes, then add the trail and rub through a sieve. Line a basin with suet paste rolled thin, put in the snipe, the sauce and some truffles; cover the top with paste, steam 1½ hours, and serve hot.

MISS WALDER, HORSHAM

MUSHROOMS FOR DINNER

MUSHROOMS are in great demand not only to make Mushroom soups, in the evening, but to flavour the more sophisticated and elaborate dishes prepared for dinner, the more important meal of the day. Hence the choice of recipes given in this Section, many of which are suitable for the more ceremonial occasions.

MUSHROOM SOUP 1 quart fresh mushrooms   2 oz. flour
2 oz. butter   ¼ pint cream

Wash, but do not peel, the mushrooms; put them in water with a dash of vinegar in it, bring to the boil, and then simmer slowly until the mushrooms are soft enough to be rubbed through a sieve. This will give you a mushroom *purée* which you will set aside and keep warm. In the meantime, put the butter in a pan over a slow fire, and as it melts, sift the flour into the pan and work it with a wooden spoon into a smooth paste; then add gradually the required quantity of hot milk and water in equal proportions, stirring all the while, over a good heat. Season with pepper and salt, and just a dusting of nutmeg; also the usual herbs (*bouquet garni*) in a muslin bag. When the soup comes to the boil, fish out the muslin bag of herbs and put into the pan the mushroom *purée*, stir well and when the soup comes to the boil again, add the cream, stir well in and serve. Small square pieces of stale bread fried in fat added to the soup are an improvement.

GREEN EGGS Cooked spinach   Minced parsley
Butter   Onion juice
Salt and pepper   Eggs
Fried croûtons   Slices of ham
White sauce
1 or 2 finely chopped mushrooms

Having cooked and chopped or sieved the spinach,

nicely seasoned with salt, pepper and butter or cream, add to it sufficient rich white sauce to make about 2 cupfuls in all. Take small ramekins, butter them well, place a little chopped parsley, a drop or two of onion juice and a teaspoonful of finely chopped mushrooms, previously gently cooked in a little butter with salt in each ramekin and, on this, break an egg, seasoning with salt and pepper. Put the cases in a pan containing hot water, and cook gently in the oven until the eggs are set but not hard. Dish up the hot spinach in an entrée dish; on this set the croûtes of fried bread and carefully turn an egg on to each round. Serve with slices of mild ham as an entrée or supper dish.

VOL-AU-VENT SURPRISE

2 lb. potatoes
1 oz. butter
½ lb. mushrooms
For Kidneys:
  Salt and pepper
  Dusting of flour
  1 pint good rich stock
  Breadcrumbs

Salt and pepper
2 egg yolks
3 kidneys

1 egg yolk
1 oz. butter
Butter

To prepare potatoes, boil them until tender, drain well and dry out thoroughly on side of fire. Mash, adding salt and pepper and egg yolks, well beaten, with the butter. Cool a little, then turn this mixture out on to a floured pastry-board. Mould with the hands into a round 'raised' pie or *vol-au-vent*, keeping back enough of the mixture to make a cover. Brush over with beaten egg and bake in a hot oven until golden brown. Peel the mushrooms and the kidneys and cut both up, then place, together, for a few moments in boiling water (or, better still, *sauté* gently in butter until tender). If boiled, drain well, add salt and pepper, the butter, flour and stock. Simmer slowly for half an hour (if the mushrooms and kidneys have been *sauté* the method is the same, simmer after they are lightly browned). When done, add the beaten yolk of egg, after removing the pan from the fire, stir well and use to fill the prepared *vol-au-vent*. Pop on the potato 'cover,' brush this also lightly over with beaten egg and brown under the grill or in a sharp oven. If wished, some cooked peas or coarsely-chopped hard-boiled eggs may also be added to filling.

CHICKEN LIVER CROUSTADES

½ cup chicken livers ½ tablespoon flour
2 tablespoons Sherry or Madeira
Baker's loaf stale bread ½ cup cream
1 cup small mushrooms Butter

Cut bread into 2-in. cubes. With a sharp knife remove centres, leaving neat box. Brush with melted butter and brown in oven. Fill with mixture: *Sauté* diced livers, sliced mushroom caps and chopped stems in butter. Sprinkle with flour, add cream and seasoning and simmer 5 minutes. Add wine, and when hot, fill the *croustades*. Garnish with a little minced parsley.

THIMBLE CLUB, MANCHESTER, NEW HAMPSHIRE

ROGNONS DE VEAU CLEMENTINE

Cut open 2 good, light-coloured veal kidneys, remove the hard core, but leave some of the fat. Salt and pepper them and cook in butter in a covered earthen casserole in a slow oven, basting frequently. After 20 minutes (or when the kidneys are three-quarters cooked) place around them 18 mushroom caps and 6 small onions previously *sauté*'d in butter to a pale gold colour. Let all this simmer 5 minutes in the fat of the kidneys, then baste the whole with 3 or 4 tablespoons of port wine and cover tightly. When the port is half reduced, blench in a teaspoon of prepared mustard (French type). Just 5 minutes more in the oven and your dish is ready to serve.

PHEANEAS BECK: '*Clémentine*' in the Kitchen

LOBSTER CHOW MIN

1 lb. boiled lobster meat 1 small onion
1 small tin bamboo shoots ½ lb. fresh mushrooms
1 tablespoonful butter ½ lb. crispy noodles
2 stalks celery Salt and cayenne
1 teaspoonful Worcester sauce
1 egg

For 'Crispy Noodles'
8 oz. flour Pinch of salt
¼ teaspoon grated nutmeg
2 egg yolks

Tinned lobster is frequently used for this dish in the States, although freshly boiled lobster is very much better. There must be a pound of the flesh when removed from shell. The bamboo shoots are, really, optional, but should be used if obtainable. Tinned ones may be purchased in England in some of the big stores. Heat the butter, add half the lobster meat, *sauté* for a few minutes, then add the finely chopped onion and celery and the mushrooms, cut into fine strips, also the bamboo shoots, if any are being used. Mix all this together, add the Worcester sauce and cook, covered, for about 10 minutes.

STUFFED LOBSTER

Boiled and cooled lobster
Good Béchamel sauce
Chopped herbs
Dusting cayenne pepper
Fresh mushrooms
Brown breadcrumbs
Butter
Cognac brandy

Cook lobster in *court-bouillon* and let it cool. Split in two very carefully without separating the head from the body, if possible. Cut the flesh into round slices. Mix the green portion of interior—the liver—and the coral, if any, with the sauce, chopped mushrooms, chopped herbs (chervil, parsley and chives), a sprinkling of brown breadcrumbs, salt and pepper, adding a touch of cayenne, if liked. Use this mixture to fill the half shells and brown in a hot oven for a few minutes; then cover each surface with the pieces of lobster, one round overlapping the other. Sprinkle with a little Cognac Brandy, spread with a layer of nicely seasoned Béchamel, dot with butter, heat well through in a quick oven and serve at once.

RED MULLET WITH MUSHROOMS

Butter an earthenware or glass casserole, and put in it a cleaned and scaled Red Mullet, with about a tablespoonful of butter, some pepper and salt and a little chopped parsley. Cook gently, turning the fish carefully once during the operation, and keeping the pan covered. Peel some small mushrooms and simmer them in just enough white wine to cover, adding a little parsley, chervil, tarragon and chives, as well as a little butter. When the mushrooms are done, add them to the fish and continue to simmer fish and mushrooms together until the sauce is well blended. Serve hot straight from the casserole.

SOLE AMBASSADRICE

A poached Sole served whole with a *Sauce Normande* to which minced mushrooms and poached oysters have been added.

SOLE BONNE FEMME Cook together in butter some minced mushrooms, a chopped shallot, and some parsley, salt, pepper and lemon juice. Cook a sole slowly in white wine and an equal quantity of velouté made with fish stock in a small braising pan or a casserole. When cooked, remove the fish and keep hot, reduce the sauce somewhat, add some butter and the yolk of an egg or two; mix in the mushrooms, etc. Arrange the sauce over the fish and put under the grill or into a hot oven for three or four minutes before serving.
SIR FRANCIS COLCHESTER-WEMYSS:
The Pleasures of the Table, 1931

SOLE NORMANDE

1 large sole
1 pint fresh mussels
12 oysters
$\frac{1}{2}$ pint shrimps
Flour
$\frac{1}{2}$ cup thick cream

White wine
Salt and pepper
Butter
$\frac{1}{2}$ lb. mushrooms
1 shallot

Have the sole filleted. Open the mussels over the fire and set liquor aside, removing mussels. Open the oysters, carefully straining their liquor and setting that, too, aside. Peel some fine shrimps, setting aside the shells and heads. Place about one cupful of white wine with the same amount of water in a small saucepan. Add to this the head and bones of the sole, the heads and shells of the shrimps, the liquor from mussels and oysters, salt, pepper, the shallot and the butter in which the sliced mushrooms have been gently cooked. Cook all this slowly for half an hour then strain through muslin. Re-heat and use to poach the fillets of sole until done—which will take about 10 to 12 minutes' gentle cooking. Remove fillets and lay them in a buttered baking dish, longways. Mix a couple of ounces of flour with the same amount of heated butter, as when making an ordinary white sauce, moisten with the strained extract of fish and cook for five minutes gently, then add cream and see that the seasoning is as it should be. Pour this over the fillets of sole, decorating with mushrooms, shrimps, mussels and oysters, nicely arranged to form a border. Pass under the flame of a gas griller or in a Dutch oven to colour surface slightly, and serve in cooking dish. This is the sole *par excellence*.

Sole cooked whole in a baking dish, in the oven, with some butter, a fish *fumet* and some mushroom *purée:* serve in the liquor in which it was cooked; add a squeeze of lemon at the last moment. **SOLE AU PLAT**

A poached sole garnished with tomatoes and mushrooms, some shallots, garlic and parsley chopped finely and cooked in olive oil; serve with a sprinkling of capers and some chopped parsely. **SOLE PROVENCALE**

A sole poached in red wine with chopped shallots and mushrooms; it is served with mushrooms and small onions, and in its own liquor as sauce. **SOLE BOURGUIGNONNE**

Fillets of sole poached, stuffed and folded crownwise; garnish with poached soft herring roes, slices of truffles and small mushrooms; cover with a white sauce before serving. **SOLE CAREME**

Fillets of sole poached in red wine, garnished with small mushrooms, little onions, fish *quenelles* and slices of truffles; serve with a *Sauce Chambord*. **SOLE CHAMBORD**

A sole cooked whole in a baking dish with a fish *fumet* and white wine; mushrooms, shallots and *Fines herbes:* serve with a *Velouté*. **SOLE COQUELIN**

Rather large trout, filleted	Fresh mushrooms	**FILETS DE TRUITE VAUCLUSIENNE**
White wine	1 chopped truffle	
Crayfish, boiled	Salt and cayenne	
Thick Béchamel sauce	1 beaten egg	
Egg yolks	Butter	
Lemon juice	Deep fat for frying	
Brown, fine breadcrumbs		

This is a somewhat sophisticated entirely delicious recipe. Boil the fillets of trout in white wine, or, rather, poach them in it. When done, remove, drain, and cut into rather large triangular pieces. Shell the boiled crayfish, keeping claws aside, after cracking neatly. Cut the tail portion of these miniature lobsters into small dice, mix with chopped mushrooms, the truffle and sufficient thick *Béchamel* to bind the mixture to a thick paste. The *Béchamel* should have been thickened by the addition of one or more egg yolks and flavoured with lemon juice, salt and cayenne to taste. Spread the mixture on each triangle of fish, coating evenly and pressing flat with a palette knife. Dip each piece of fish thus prepared first into beaten egg, then in breadcrumbs, allow surface to harden, then fry a golden brown in deep fat. Serve piled on one another, the corners of each triangle being ornamented with one of the tiny crayfish claws, stuck into it at right angles. An accompanying sauce may be made with the fish stock to which is added crayfish butter at the last moment.

TURBOT BONNE FEMME In a saucepan put a level dessertspoonful of chopped shallot with a tablespoonful of melted butter. Cook gently for a few minutes, then add 3 oz. of sliced mushrooms. Simmer again for a minute or two, then add one wineglassful of white wine and two of water.

Butter a fireproof dish generously. Lay in it slices or fillets of turbot. Pour over them the contents of the saucepan, and sprinkle the fish with small pieces of butter.

Cover the dish with a piece of greased paper and set it in a moderate oven. Cook for about 30 minutes, basting several times, being careful to put back the paper after doing so.

Carefully pour off all the liquid from the fish into a saucepan. Keep the turbot hot by standing it over a large pan containing boiling water.

Thicken the liquid with a little roux and, standing it in a bain-marie, let it cook for at least five minutes. Season it, and just before you pour it back over the fish, whip in several small pieces of butter and a table-spoonful or two of cream.

MRS. LUCAS: *A Pretty Kettle of Fish*

TETE DE VEAU EN TORTUE

1 boiled (or half) calf's head	Strip red pepper
Few blades fresh basil	Stoned olives
1 tablespoon tomato purée	2 sheep's kidneys
Few button mushroom caps	Croûtons
1 cup bouillon	1 glass dry sherry
2 cups brown *roux*	Salt and pepper
1 tablespoon beef essence	1 truffle
Chopped pickled gherkins	Butter
1 or 2 hard-boiled eggs	

The sauce of this otherwise inexpensive meat dish

is in the nature of a court dress for a village maiden, and, at that, still other ingredients were called for in this old French recipe such as cocks' combs and crayfish!

Cook the head as described in preceding recipe. Now for the sauce. Place the sherry and bouillon in a saucepan with the basil. Cook fast to reduce to half original quantity, adding salt, pepper and strip of red pepper. Thicken by addition of the *roux* and the tomato purée, add beef extract, cut-up kidneys, cut-up truffle, stoned green olives, chopped gherkins and mushroom caps. Simmer all together for 15 to 20 minutes then add the head, cut into neat pieces, and simmer 10 minutes longer with more bouillon if required. Garnish dish with croûtons—rounds of hard-boiled egg, fried in butter, and . . . crayfish!

POULET SAUTE MARENGO

This old favourite way of cooking a chicken in an open pan is supposed to date from the Battle of Marengo, when, to save time, there was a *plat unique* served to Bonaparte, a chicken cooked in olive oil together with some eggs fried in the same oil and crayfish as well. The chicken and eggs cooked in oil are probably the only true part of the story, and we are inclined to believe that the tomato sauce and the *écrevisses* were additions to later editions of the dish. Here is Escoffier's recipe for it:

Sauter the chicken in butter and olive oil. Add a glassful of white wine, a dozen mushroom caps cooked in olive oil, just a little garlic, $1\frac{1}{2}$ cupfuls of *demi-glace* (meat gravy) with a few spoonfuls of tomato sauce added to it.

When the chicken is cooked, dress it in a deep dish, pour over it the sauce and the mushrooms and place round it four *croûtons taillés en coeur* (pieces of bread cut the shape of a heart) and fried in butter, four fried eggs, four *écrevisses* (crayfish) cooked in a *court-bouillon*: dust the lot with a pinch of chopped parsley.

POULET SAUTE PORTUGAISE

1 chicken
$\frac{1}{2}$ oz. butter
Savoury rice
2 shallots
1 gill brown veal stock

3 tomatoes
6 mushrooms
$\frac{1}{2}$ gill white wine
1 gill tomato sauce
$\frac{1}{4}$ gill oil

1 teaspoonful chicken glaze
Salt and pepper and some chopped parsley

Cut the chicken into joints, chop the shallots, and slice the mushrooms. Put the butter and oil into a stewpan. As soon as it is hot, add the chicken, and fry it a light brown colour. Then add the shallots and cook a little longer. Now put in the mushrooms, the wine, stock, tomato sauce and the chicken glaze. Cover with the lid, and put it in the oven for half-an hour to cook gently. Dish up the chicken on a hot dish, pour the sauce over, garnish round with the tomatoes cut in halves and filled with rice. Sprinkle over a little chopped parsley, and serve. Time required 1 hour. Seasonable at all times. Sufficient for four or five persons.

M. A. FAIRCLOUGH: *The Ideal Cookery Book*

STUFFED LAMB CHOPS

Thick lamb loin chops   Salt and pepper
1 or 2 chicken's livers   1 or 2 fresh mushrooms

The chops must be not less than 1½ to 2 in. thick, one bone, or even two if lamb is small, having been removed. Split the lean part of the meat in half, cutting to bone. Peel off skin. Chop the livers and peeled mushrooms and *sauté* in butter, seasoning well, until done but not browned. Use to stuff incision in chops, sew up with large needle and coarse thread, sprinkle with salt, pepper and place on a greased griller, under a hot flame or over a clear charcoal fire. Brown on both sides, remove thread and serve very hot. If preferred, once the chops have been stuffed, egg and breadcrumb them, then bake in a hot oven after placing a little butter on top of each chop. Turn once to brown other side.

LAMB CUTLETS   Lamb cutlets may be cut 'single' or 'double,' and they are really best plainly and lightly grilled, that is if from a young, freshly killed well-fed lamb, so rarely obtainable in these days of rationing and refrigeration. It is then that Mushrooms are priceless, however costly they happen to be at the time. The three best methods as recognized by the *Cuisine Classique*, for preparing lamb cutlets with mushrooms, are the following:

grilled and served with grilled tomatoes, mushrooms and bacon. **BARMAN**

dipped in egg-and-breadcrumbs mixed with finely-chopped truffles, pan-fried and served with creamed mushrooms. **BROSSARD**

dipped in egg-and-breadcrumbs, pan-fried in butter and served with a *purée* of mushrooms. **MONTROUGE**

Soak a fillet of beef (larded) in a marinade of white wine, olive oil and spices for 48 hours. Roast it in a very hot oven 20 minutes to the pound. Take it out, take off fat and add a little of the marinade to the gravy. Let it reduce. Add the juice of a lemon and strain it on a garniture of diced truffles, pistachios, tiny mushrooms and small olives, which have been previously blanced. Pour sauce over the fillet, let it simmer for a few minutes and before serving sprinkle meat with chopped parsley. **FILET DE BŒUF BRESSANNE**
MARY PICKFORD, HOLLYWOOD, CAL.

Middle piece of a fillet of beef	Butter
Salt and pepper	Larding bacon

FILET DE BŒUF MADERE

Roasting spits being no longer in everyday use—more's the pity!—the centre portion of a fine fillet of beef must perforce be oven-baked. Trim, shape and tie up neatly after larding the meat in regular rows as described in 'Boeuf à la mode' recipe. Be sure the oven is *very* hot before putting in the meat so that the surface is quickly browned. For under-done meat, which is best, allow 15 to 20 minutes per lb. Baste well while cooking and, when done, use the gravy as a foundation for the *Sauce Madère*. Mushrooms and thin slices of truffle are the classical accompaniment and garnish of this sauce, which should be handed round, *not* poured over the roast fillet.

Individual tournedos of beef	Salt and pepper
2 or 3 tablespoons good stock	Chopped parsley
1 scanty teaspoon potato flour	1 or 2 shallots
3 or 4 fresh mushrooms	Butter
1 small glass white wine	
1 teaspoon tomato *purée*	

TOURNEDOS CHASSEUR

Pan-fry the *tournedos* and keep hot. Fry chopped

shallots and mushrooms in butter, without colouring. Moisten with wine, simmer to reduce a little, then add stock, previously blended with potato flour (*fécule*) and tomato *purée*. Season well, roll the *tournedos* in this sauce, without allowing to cook longer, and serve at once, sprinkling with finely-chopped parsley.

TOURNEDOS DAUPHINOISE

½ lb. fresh mushrooms
1 dessertspoon flour
Individual tournedos
Fried croûtons
2 tablespoons butter
½ cup thick cream
Salt and pepper

First prepare the mushrooms *à la crème*. Slice, after peeling and *sauté* in butter, until all liquid has evaporated and butter is clear; then reduce heat, add the cream previously blended with the flour, season well and keep hot while the *tournedos* are being grilled. Use their drippings as gravy to make the sauce. To serve, turn the mushroom *purée* into a hot dish, add as many fried *croûtons* as there are *tournedos*, placing one *tournedos* on each *croûton:* pour the gravy or sauce over them and serve hot.

RUMPSTEAK A LA HUSSARDE

2 lb. lean rumpsteak
2 tablespoons chopped onion
3 oz. calf's liver
3 oz. stale breadcrumbs
1 pint consommé or good stock
A little milk
6 tablespoons butter
Salt and pepper
¼ lb. mushrooms
2 egg yolks

Select a thick, square piece of meat. Chop the liver finely. Soak the breadcrumbs in a little milk and squeeze dry. Mix with the liver, the onions, salt and pepper. Mix all this thoroughly and brown in a couple of tablespoons of butter. Allow stuffing to cool, then mix with the egg yolks and set aside.

Taking a very sharp knife, cut the piece of steak into slices, without, however, separating them entirely. There should be four or five 'pages' of them, in between which some of the stuffing must be spread, not allowing it to come nearer than half an inch of the edges. When ready, tie up securely but not too tightly or the stuffing will be pressed out. Brown this prepared square of meat in the rest of the butter, on all sides; salt again and when nicely coloured moisten gradually with the consommé or stock. Add the mushroom caps and any of the left-over stuffing. Cover closely and allow dish to simmer very gently for about four hours. Serve with mashed potatoes.

1½ lb. fillet of veal	4 tablespoons butter	**FILLETS OF VEAL**
1 shallot	4 mushrooms	**TALLEYRAND**
1 gill rich white sauce	2 egg yolks	
Salt and pepper	Lemon juice	

Cut the meat into about 8 fillets or steaks, flatten them out nicely, then brown them lightly in heated butter, seasoning to taste with salt and pepper. They must be very lightly coloured, if at all. Remove meat and keep hot. Chop the shallot and the mushrooms, first browning the former in the hot butter then, when nearly done, adding the mushrooms, cooking gently together until done. Strain off butter. Heat the white sauce, stir in the shallot and mushrooms, remove pan from fire and beat in the egg yolks. Season with salt, pepper and lemon juice as wished, adding also, if required, a small pinch of chopped parsley. Reheat carefully, taking care the sauce does not boil. Serve the fillets of veal on a bed of mashed potatoes and pour sauce over the meat.

| 2 young partridges | Butter | **PERDREAUX EN** |
| Brown mushroom sauce | Thin slices fat salt pork | **PAPILLOTES** |

Cut each bird in two and brown delicately in butter. When almost done, remove and wrap each half in the slices of fat pork, then in oiled paper. Grill gently for about 20 minutes, turning frequently and taking care the paper does not burn. Remove paper when birds are done and serve them very hot, pouring the sauce over them. The ordinary brown mushroom sauce should be enriched by the addition of the butter in which the partridges are first cooked and a little good dry white wine. It should be gently reduced by slow cooking and really ought to be made well in advance of the cooking of the birds in order that it may mellow properly.

1 Pheasant	2 oz. of butter	**ROAST PHEASANT**
Some fat bacon for larding	Salt and cayenne	**WITH MUSHROOMS**
1 dozen mushrooms		

Prepare the pheasant in the usual way, then lard it

along each side of the breast with small lardoons of bacon. Wash and skin the mushrooms; if large, cut them into halves or quarters. Stuff the pheasant with them; also add 1 ounce of butter, $\frac{1}{2}$ teaspoonful of salt, a few grains of cayenne. Truss it neatly, and cover the whole breast with a thickly buttered piece of paper. Let it roast for half an hour, basting several times. Remove the paper and roast ten minutes longer. Serve with gravy and bread sauce.

MRS. BLACK'S *Superior Cookery*

MUSHROOMS FOR SUPPER

MUSHROOM TARTS

Fresh mushrooms	1 egg
Butter	Flour
Sour cream	Short pastry crust
Finely-chopped chicken	Milk

Having prepared the mushrooms for cooking, fry them gently in butter after rolling each lightly in flour. When done, chop them coarsely, add the chopped chicken—cold left-over will do, or ham or cold roast veal—and add sufficient sour cream to bind the mixture. Season rather highly. Roll out the pastry rather thinly and cut into rounds the size of a small teacup. Pile a spoonful of the chicken and mushroom mixture in the centre of one round of pastry, moisten edges and cover with another round of pastry, pressing edges well together. Brush surface of each tartlet with the beaten egg yolk mixed with a little milk. Bake in a sharp oven until brown and serve hot with tomato or any suitable sauce. If preferred, leave *sauté* mushrooms whole, pile meat mixture in centre and cut out the pastry rounds large enough to enclose the mushrooms, proceeding otherwise as indicated. NOTE. Add the butter and gravy from *sauté* mushrooms to the sauce accompanying this delicious light supper dish.

MUSHROOMS SOUS CLOCHE Creamed Mushrooms served piping hot in the individual fireproof glass dishes, with a glass 'cloche' cover, in which they were cooked.

A CATALOGUE OF SELECTED DOVER BOOKS
IN ALL FIELDS OF INTEREST

A CATALOGUE OF SELECTED DOVER BOOKS IN ALL FIELDS OF INTEREST

CELESTIAL OBJECTS FOR COMMON TELESCOPES, T. W. Webb. The most used book in amateur astronomy: inestimable aid for locating and identifying nearly 4,000 celestial objects. Edited, updated by Margaret W. Mayall. 77 illustrations. Total of 645pp. 5⅜ x 8½.
20917-2, 20918-0 Pa., Two-vol. set $9.00

HISTORICAL STUDIES IN THE LANGUAGE OF CHEMISTRY, M. P. Crosland. The important part language has played in the development of chemistry from the symbolism of alchemy to the adoption of systematic nomenclature in 1892. ". . . wholeheartedly recommended,"—Science. 15 illustrations. 416pp. of text. 5⅝ x 8¼. 63702-6 Pa. $6.00

BURNHAM'S CELESTIAL HANDBOOK, Robert Burnham, Jr. Thorough, readable guide to the stars beyond our solar system. Exhaustive treatment, fully illustrated. Breakdown is alphabetical by constellation: Andromeda to Cetus in Vol. 1; Chamaeleon to Orion in Vol. 2; and Pavo to Vulpecula in Vol. 3. Hundreds of illustrations. Total of about 2000pp. 6⅛ x 9¼.
23567-X, 23568-8, 23673-0 Pa., Three-vol. set $27.85

THEORY OF WING SECTIONS: INCLUDING A SUMMARY OF AIRFOIL DATA, Ira H. Abbott and A. E. von Doenhoff. Concise compilation of subatomic aerodynamic characteristics of modern NASA wing sections, plus description of theory. 350pp. of tables. 693pp. 5⅜ x 8½.
60586-8 Pa. $8.50

DE RE METALLICA, Georgius Agricola. Translated by Herbert C. Hoover and Lou H. Hoover. The famous Hoover translation of greatest treatise on technological chemistry, engineering, geology, mining of early modern times (1556). All 289 original woodcuts. 638pp. 6¾ x 11.
60006-8 Clothbd. $17.95

THE ORIGIN OF CONTINENTS AND OCEANS, Alfred Wegener. One of the most influential, most controversial books in science, the classic statement for continental drift. Full 1966 translation of Wegener's final (1929) version. 64 illustrations. 246pp. 5⅜ x 8½. 61708-4 Pa. $4.50

THE PRINCIPLES OF PSYCHOLOGY, William James. Famous long course complete, unabridged. Stream of thought, time perception, memory, experimental methods; great work decades ahead of its time. Still valid, useful; read in many classes. 94 figures. Total of 1391pp. 5⅜ x 8½.
20381-6, 20382-4 Pa., Two-vol. set $13.00

CATALOGUE OF DOVER BOOKS

AMERICAN BIRD ENGRAVINGS, Alexander Wilson et al. All 76 plates. from Wilson's *American Ornithology* (1808-14), most important ornithological work before Audubon, plus 27 plates from the supplement (1825-33) by Charles Bonaparte. Over 250 birds portrayed. 8 plates also reproduced in full color. 111pp. 9⅜ x 12½. 23195-X Pa. $6.00

CRUICKSHANK'S PHOTOGRAPHS OF BIRDS OF AMERICA, Allan D. Cruickshank. Great ornithologist, photographer presents 177 closeups, groupings, panoramas, flightings, etc., of about 150 different birds. Expanded *Wings in the Wilderness*. Introduction by Helen G. Cruickshank. 191pp. 8¼ x 11. 23497-5 Pa. $6.00

AMERICAN WILDLIFE AND PLANTS, A. C. Martin, et al. Describes food habits of more than 1000 species of mammals, birds, fish. Special treatment of important food plants. Over 300 illustrations. 500pp. 5⅜ x 8½. 20793-5 Pa. $4.95

THE PEOPLE CALLED SHAKERS, Edward D. Andrews. Lifetime of research, definitive study of Shakers: origins, beliefs, practices, dances, social organization, furniture and crafts, impact on 19th-century USA, present heritage. Indispensable to student of American history, collector. 33 illustrations. 351pp. 5⅜ x 8½. 21081-2 Pa. $4.50

OLD NEW YORK IN EARLY PHOTOGRAPHS, Mary Black. New York City as it was in 1853-1901, through 196 wonderful photographs from N.-Y. Historical Society. Great Blizzard, Lincoln's funeral procession, great buildings. 228pp. 9 x 12. 22907-6 Pa. $8.95

MR. LINCOLN'S CAMERA MAN: MATHEW BRADY, Roy Meredith. Over 300 Brady photos reproduced directly from original negatives, photos. Jackson, Webster, Grant, Lee, Carnegie, Barnum; Lincoln; Battle Smoke, Death of Rebel Sniper, Atlanta Just After Capture. Lively commentary. 368pp. 8⅜ x 11¼. 23021-X Pa. $8.95

TRAVELS OF WILLIAM BARTRAM, William Bartram. From 1773-8, Bartram explored Northern Florida, Georgia, Carolinas, and reported on wild life, plants, Indians, early settlers. Basic account for period, entertaining reading. Edited by Mark Van Doren. 13 illustrations. 141pp. 5⅜ x 8½. 20013-2 Pa. $5.00

THE GENTLEMAN AND CABINET MAKER'S DIRECTOR, Thomas Chippendale. Full reprint, 1762 style book, most influential of all time; chairs, tables, sofas, mirrors, cabinets, etc. 200 plates, plus 24 photographs of surviving pieces. 249pp. 9⅞ x 12¾. 21601-2 Pa. $7.95

AMERICAN CARRIAGES, SLEIGHS, SULKIES AND CARTS, edited by Don H. Berkebile. 168 Victorian illustrations from catalogues, trade journals, fully captioned. Useful for artists. Author is Assoc. Curator, Div. of Transportation of Smithsonian Institution. 168pp. 8½ x 9½. 23328-6 Pa. $5.00

CATALOGUE OF DOVER BOOKS

THE COMPLETE BOOK OF DOLL MAKING AND COLLECTING, Catherine Christopher. Instructions, patterns for dozens of dolls, from rag doll on up to elaborate, historically accurate figures. Mould faces, sew clothing, make doll houses, etc. Also collecting information. Many illustrations. 288pp. 6 x 9. 22066-4 Pa. $4.50

THE DAGUERREOTYPE IN AMERICA, Beaumont Newhall. Wonderful portraits, 1850's townscapes, landscapes; full text plus 104 photographs. The basic book. Enlarged 1976 edition. 272pp. 8¼ x 11¼.
23322-7 Pa. $7.95

CRAFTSMAN HOMES, Gustav Stickley. 296 architectural drawings, floor plans, and photographs illustrate 40 different kinds of "Mission-style" homes from *The Craftsman* (1901-16), voice of American style of simplicity and organic harmony. Thorough coverage of Craftsman idea in text and picture, now collector's item. 224pp. 8⅛ x 11. 23791-5 Pa. $6.00

PEWTER-WORKING: INSTRUCTIONS AND PROJECTS, Burl N. Osborn. & Gordon O. Wilber. Introduction to pewter-working for amateur craftsman. History and characteristics of pewter; tools, materials, step-by-step instructions. Photos, line drawings, diagrams. Total of 160pp. 7⅞ x 10¾. 23786-9 Pa. $3.50

THE GREAT CHICAGO FIRE, edited by David Lowe. 10 dramatic, eye-witness accounts of the 1871 disaster, including one of the aftermath and rebuilding, plus 70 contemporary photographs and illustrations of the ruins—courthouse, Palmer House, Great Central Depot, etc. Introduction by David Lowe. 87pp. 8¼ x 11. 23771-0 Pa. $4.00

SILHOUETTES: A PICTORIAL ARCHIVE OF VARIED ILLUSTRATIONS, edited by Carol Belanger Grafton. Over 600 silhouettes from the 18th to 20th centuries include profiles and full figures of men and women, children, birds and animals, groups and scenes, nature, ships, an alphabet. Dozens of uses for commercial artists and craftspeople. 144pp. 8⅜ x 11¼.
23781-8 Pa. $4.50

ANIMALS: 1,419 COPYRIGHT-FREE ILLUSTRATIONS OF MAMMALS, BIRDS, FISH, INSECTS, ETC., edited by Jim Harter. Clear wood engravings present, in extremely lifelike poses, over 1,000 species of animals. One of the most extensive copyright-free pictorial sourcebooks of its kind. Captions. Index. 284pp. 9 x 12. 23766-4 Pa. $8.95

INDIAN DESIGNS FROM ANCIENT ECUADOR, Frederick W. Shaffer. 282 original designs by pre-Columbian Indians of Ecuador (500-1500 A.D.). Designs include people, mammals, birds, reptiles, fish, plants, heads, geometric designs. Use as is or alter for advertising, textiles, leathercraft, etc. Introduction. 95pp. 8¾ x 11¼. 23764-8 Pa. $3.50

SZIGETI ON THE VIOLIN, Joseph Szigeti. Genial, loosely structured tour by premier violinist, featuring a pleasant mixture of reminiscenes, insights into great music and musicians, innumerable tips for practicing violinists. 385 musical passages. 256pp. 5⅝ x 8¼. 23763-X Pa. $4.00

CATALOGUE OF DOVER BOOKS

AMERICAN ANTIQUE FURNITURE, Edgar G. Miller, Jr. The basic coverage of all American furniture before 1840: chapters per item chronologically cover all types of furniture, with more than 2100 photos. Total of 1106pp. 7⅞ x 10¾.   21599-7, 21600-4 Pa., Two-vol. set $17.90

ILLUSTRATED GUIDE TO SHAKER FURNITURE, Robert Meader. Director, Shaker Museum, Old Chatham, presents up-to-date coverage of all furniture and appurtenances, with much on local styles not available elsewhere. 235 photos. 146pp. 9 x 12.   22819-3 Pa. $6.00

ORIENTAL RUGS, ANTIQUE AND MODERN, Walter A. Hawley. Persia, Turkey, Caucasus, Central Asia, China, other traditions. Best general survey of all aspects: styles and periods, manufacture, uses, symbols and their interpretation, and identification. 96 illustrations, 11 in color. 320pp. 6⅛ x 9¼.   22366-3 Pa. $6.95

CHINESE POTTERY AND PORCELAIN, R. L. Hobson. Detailed descriptions and analyses by former Keeper of the Department of Oriental Antiquities and Ethnography at the British Museum. Covers hundreds of pieces from primitive times to 1915. Still the standard text for most periods. 136 plates, 40 in full color. Total of 750pp. 5⅜ x 8½.
23253-0 Pa. $10.00

THE WARES OF THE MING DYNASTY, R. L. Hobson. Foremost scholar examines and illustrates many varieties of Ming (1368-1644). Famous blue and white, polychrome, lesser-known styles and shapes. 117 illustrations, 9 full color, of outstanding pieces. Total of 263pp. 6⅛ x 9¼. (Available in U.S. only)   23652-8 Pa. $6.00

Prices subject to change without notice.

Available at your book dealer or write for free catalogue to Dept. GI, Dover Publications, Inc., 31 East Second Street, Mineola, N.Y. 11501. Dover publishes more than 175 books each year on science, elementary and advanced mathematics, biology, music, art, literary history, social sciences and other areas.